MW01118056

A Joke-A-Day Book

By Gyles Brandreth
Illustrated by Shelagh McGee

WINGS BOOKS
New York / Avenel, New Jersey

Copyright (c) 1979 by Sterling Publishing Company, Inc.

Originally published in 1978 under the title *Jokes! Jokes!! Jokes!!!*
by Corgi Books, a division of Transworld Publishers Ltd.,
text copyright (c) 1978 by Gyles Brandreth,
illustration copyright (c) 1978 by Transworld Publishers Ltd.

All rights reserved.

This 1992 edition is published by Wings Books,
distributed by Outlet Book Company,
a Random House Company, 40 Engelhard Avenue,
Avenel, New Jersey, 07001, by arrangement with
Sterling Publishing Company, Inc.

Printed and Bound in the United States of America

Library of Congress Cataloging-in-Publication Data

Brandreth, Gyles Daubeney, 1948-
[Jokes, jokes, jokes]
A joke-a-day book / by Gyles Brandreth ; illustrated by Shelagh McGee.
p. cm.
First published in 1978 under the title: jokes, jokes, jokes!.
Originally published: New York : Sterling Pub. Co., 1979.
ISBN 0-517-07766-3
1. Wit and humor, Juvenile. 2. Jokes--Calenders. I. Title
[PN6163.B7155 1992]
828'.91402--dc20 91-37921
CIP

8 7 6 5 4 3 2 1

THIS BOOK IS DEDICATED TO THE MEMORY OF
MY GOOD FRIENDS*

Ida Hope
May Morning
Annie Seedball
Astrid de Stars
Ken John Peel
Luke Warm and
Eva Drawsoff

(*They'd still be alive if they hadn't read the manuscript of this book. Unfortunately, they all died laughing.)

January

1 Did you hear about the Prince who was kissed by a beautiful young girl at a New Year's Eve party?

2 **NEWS FLASH:**
The marriage of two lighthouse keepers is on the rocks.

3 What did Tarzan say when he saw the elephants coming?

"Here come the elephants!"

4 What did Tarzan say when he saw the elephants coming wearing dark glasses?

Nothing. He didn't recognize them.

5 **QUESTION OF THE WEEK:**
What begins with T and ends with T and is full of T?

6 **Father:** I've stopped our Willy from biting his nails.
Mother: *Oh, how did you do it?*
Father: I knocked all his teeth out.

7 Why do little birds in a nest always agree?

He turned into a toad.

New Year's Day

ANSWER OF THE WEEK:
A teapot!

Twelfth Night

Because they don't want to fall out.

January

8 Did you hear about the musician who spent all his time in bed?

9 **Max:** Where does a frog hang his overcoat?

Mini: *In a croakroom!*

10 I walked into a hardware shop the other day and asked the clerk if he had one-inch nails. He said he had. That was lucky because my back was itching and I needed someone to scratch it.

11 Around the world today, people of all colors—especially green and orange—will dress up as jello and race to see who is Mother Earth's fastest-ever jello.

World Jello Day

12 How do you start a flea race?

13 Why can the world never come to an end?

14 When do broken bones become useful?

When they begin to knit!

National Beets Day

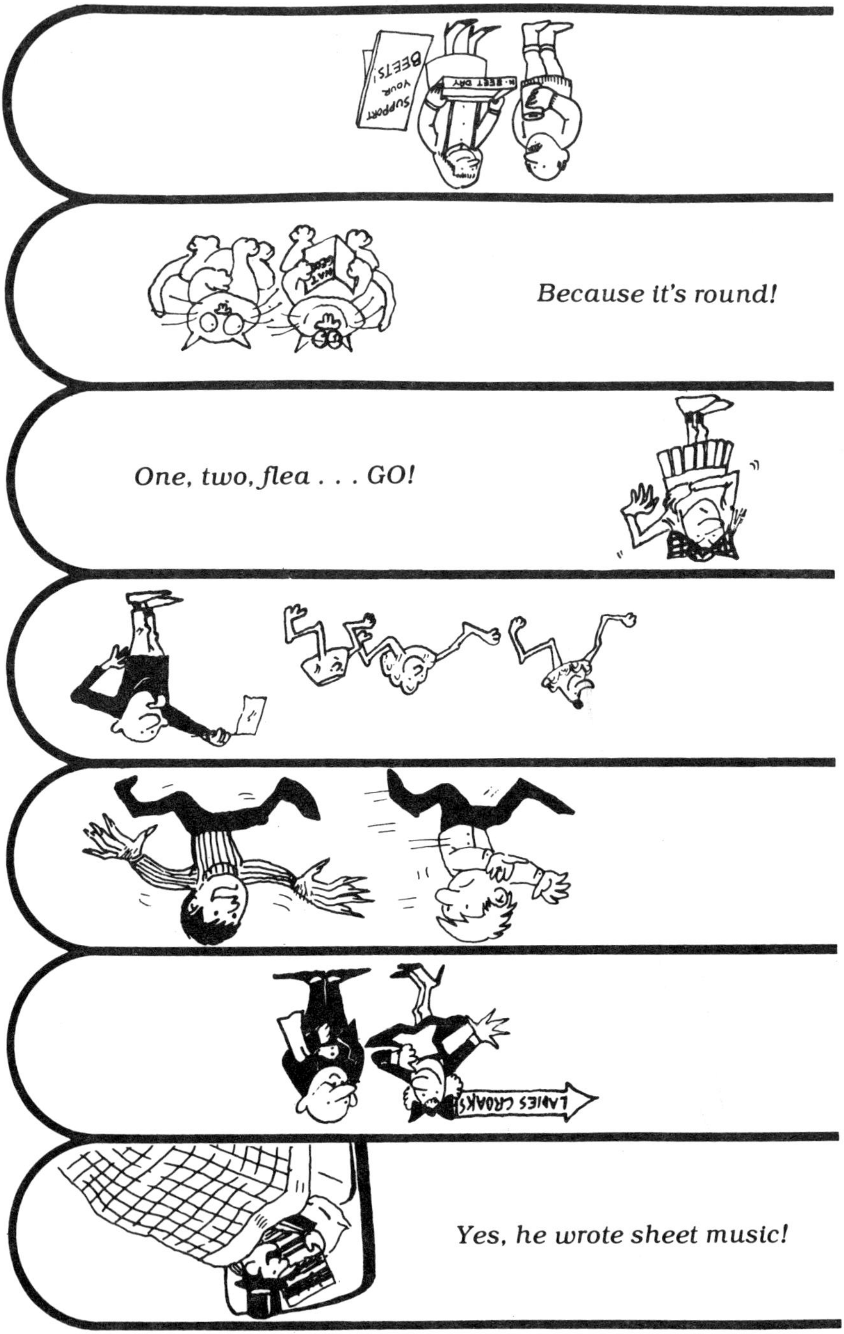
SUPPORT YOUR BEETS!
BEET DAY
Because it's round!
NAT GEO
One, two, flea . . . GO!
LADIES CROAKS
Yes, he wrote sheet music!

January

15

There are three inventions that have helped people get up in the world; do you know what they are?

The elevator, the escalator and the alarm clock!

16

Jack: I'm sorry to hear your factory burned down. What did you manufacture?
Dick: *Fire extinguishers.*

National Nothing Day

17

Jill: Do you know what you look like with your eyes shut?
Jane: *No.*
Jill: Well, have a look in the mirror with your eyes shut.

18

What's the difference between a gossip and an umbrella?

19

SAYING OF THE WEEK:
My husband is so simple he even takes a saddle and riding hat to bed with him in case of nightmares.

20

I wouldn't say I was stupid, but when I went to see a mindreader he gave me my money back.

21

Lucy: How can you tell that I'm a secret agent?
John: *I don't know. How can you?*
Lucy: Because I've got a code in the head!

Martin Luther King's Birthday

Ben Franklin's Birthday

You can shut up an umbrella!

January

22

Bill: I hear the men are striking. What for?
Ben: *Shorter hours.*
Bill: Oh good. I always felt sixty minutes was too long for an hour.

23

Man: Good morning, Madam. I'm the piano tuner.
Mrs. Payne: *But I didn't send for you.*
Man: No, but your neighbors did.

24

NEWS FLASH:
The Chairman of the Blotto Blotting Paper Company announced that he would not be retiring this year after all. He said he found his work totally absorbing.

25

POLICE NOTICE:
Would the motorist who turned off the highway kindly turn it back on.

26

RIDDLE OF THE WEEK:
When is an unsharpened pencil like a bad joke?

27

John: Why are feet like ancient tales?

Jack: *Because they are leg-ends.*

28

How do you think Jack Frost gets to work?

When it has no point.

By icicle, I suppose.

January

29 What's vast and green and has a trunk?

30 How do you make a Swiss roll?

The easiest way is to push him down the side of an Alp!

31 Did you hear about the world's tiniest sailor? He was so small that he always slept on his watch.

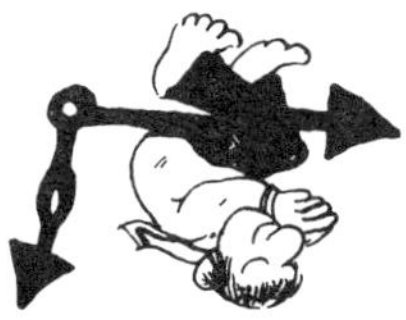

An unripe elephant.

February

1

There were two men playing Scrabble. They played ten games and each man won nine games.
But that's impossible!
No, it isn't. They were playing different people.

2

Why does an elephant have a trunk?

So that it has somewhere to hide when it sees a mouse.

Ground Hog Day

3

Did you hear about the neurotic octopus?

It was a crazy, mixed-up squid!

4

The lawyer was reading Albert's will and reached the last sentence. "And I always said I would mention my dear wife Doris in my will," read the lawyer. "So, hi there Doris!"

5

What falls in winter but never gets hurt?

6

Did you hear about the race between the cabbage, the faucet, and the tomato? The cabbage was ahead, the faucet was running slowly and the tomato was trying to ketchup!

7

Does this train stop in Chicago?

Well, there's going to be a pretty big crash if it doesn't.

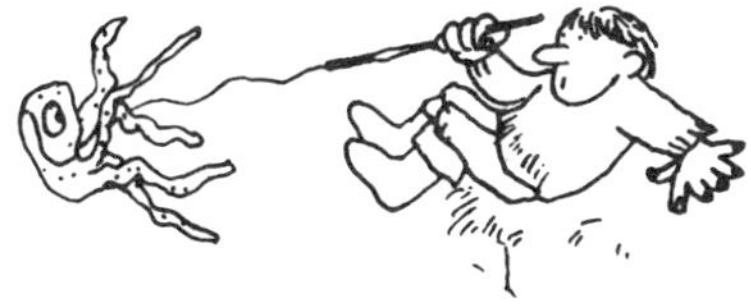

Snow!

Mushroom Day

February

8

What's the difference between a lemon and a rhino?

The lemon is yellow.

World Rhino Week

9

How do you tell the difference between an elephant and a rhinoceros?

The elephant has a better memory.

10

Why did the girl rhino paint her head yellow?

She wanted to find out if blonds have more fun!

11

How can you tell when there's a rhino in your sandwich?

12

What do you give a man-eating rhino with big feet?

Plenty of room!

13

Bill: What's the difference between a lemon, a rhino, and a tube of glue?
Ben: *You can squeeze a lemon, but you can't squeeze a rhino. But what about the glue?*
Bill: I thought that's where you'd get stuck.

14

What's the difference between a strawberry and a rhinoceros?

Saint Valentine's Day

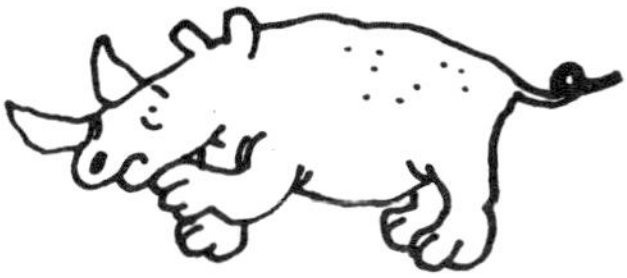

When it's too heavy to lift!

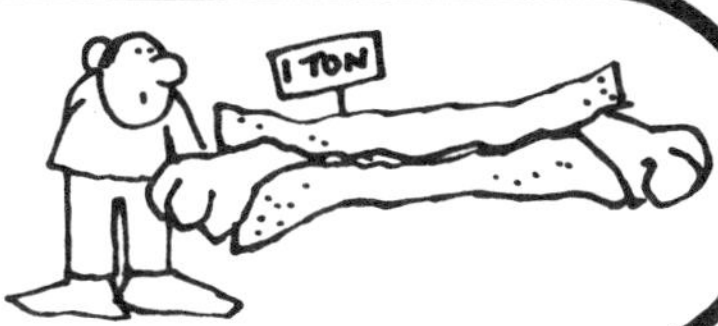

Abraham Lincoln's Birthday

A strawberry is red.

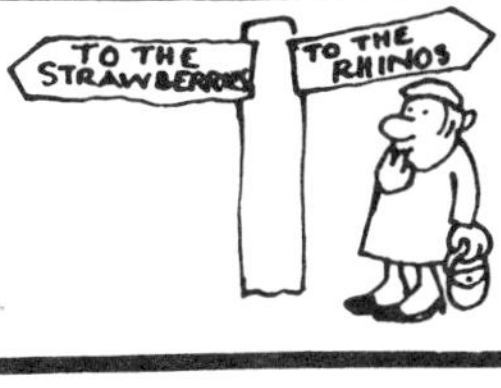

February

15 If you know a caveman or a cavewoman—or even any cavekids—today's the day to visit them and say "Hi!"

16 RIDDLE OF THE WEEK:
Why should the groom strike the bride on their wedding day?

17 NEWS FLASH:
Owing to a strike at the meteorological office, there will be no weather tomorrow.

18 Where does the elf live?

International Elves and Gnomes Day

19 **Businessman:** Get out! I can't see you today.
Salesman: *Excellent, sir. I'm selling spectacles.*

20 If you like grave humor, you might enjoy the story about the two body-snatchers. On second thought, I won't tell it. You might get carried away.

21 What was the name of the monarch with the bump on his head?

Caveperson Day

Because she's the wedding belle!

Gnome sweet gnome.

King Konk!

February

22

Collector: But this can't be George Washington's skull. It's far too small.
Dealer: *Oh, but I forgot to tell you. It was his skull when he was a little boy.*

George Washington's Birthday

23

A man went to church to get married and found the minister was planning to give him sixteen wives—four better, four worse, four richer, four poorer!

24

How do you make notes out of stone?
I don't know. How do you make notes out of stone?
You just rearrange the letters!

25

What's the difference between an Indian elephant and an African elephant?

26

What runs around all day with its sole-mate and then lies down all night with its tongue hanging out?

27

One toe turned to the other toe and whispered, "Don't look now, but there's a heel following us."

28

What is green, slippery and drinks from the wrong side of the glass?

World Hiccup Day

A grape trying to get rid of the hiccups!

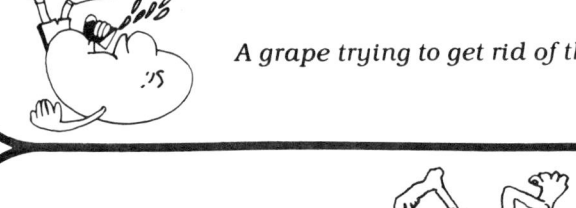

Your shoe, of course!

About 3,000 miles!

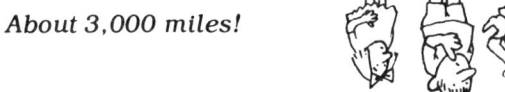

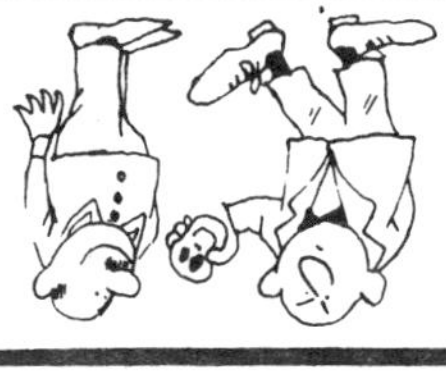

February

29

Alec: Some months have 31 days. Some months have 30 days. How many months have 28 days?
Rose: *One–February.*
Alec: No, all of them!

In Leap Years Only

March

1

IMPORTANT THINGS TO DO TODAY:
1. Give money to the baker. He kneads the dough.
2. Smile at the dry cleaner. He'll dye for you.

2

"You know, at night I snored so loudly I used to wake myself up."
"What did you do about it?"
"Now I sleep in the next room and I don't hear a thing."

3

Once upon a time this day was an internationally recognized festival. Not anymore. Fangs ain't what they used to be.

4

What was the order that General Walker gave his troops today?

"March forth!"

5

Have you heard about Will Knott? He's so lazy he signs his name "Won't."

6

When there's a bank robbery, who is always the most talkative witness?

7

Teacher: Sheila, if you worked for seventeen hours and were paid $5 for every hour you worked, what would you get?
Sheila: *A new dress.*

World Vampire Day

Stand on Your Hands Day

The teller, of course!

March

8 Today is the birthday of Gyles Brandreth, the much-loved author of this book and many other classics of contemporary literature. Birthday cards, bouquets and expensive presents should be sent to him in care of his publishers.

9 SIGN IN A COURTROOM:

Thirty days hath September, April, June, and the speeding offender!

10 How do you save a drowning mouse?

Give it mouse-to-mouse resuscitation!

11 **Customer:** What's this leathery stuff, waiter?
Waiter: *Filet of sole, sir.*
Customer: Take it away and see if you can't cut me a tender piece from the top of the boot.

12 **Editor:** Mac, did you get the story about the man who can sing bass and soprano at the same time?
Mac: *There's no story there. The man's got two heads.*

13 RIDDLE OF THE WEEK:

What pine has the longest and sharpest needles?

14 What did the earth say when it rained?

If this keeps up, my name will be mud!

The porcupine!
SLOW

March

15

I met Sam Slopps today. You know he's working for the Water Supply Board now. He's really a bit of a drip, but I asked him to drop in one day.

Buzzard Day

16

Voice on the phone: Is this the monkey house?
Zookeeper: *It is.*
Voice: Oh, good. My son's having a birthday party tomorrow and I wondered if you had any ideas for it.

17

Why is it so hard to believe in the Blarney Stone?

Because there are a lot of sham rocks in Ireland.

18

My grandmother is incredible. She's ninety-two and she hasn't got a gray hair on her head. She's totally bald.

19

What do you get when you cross a frog with a can of soda?

Croak-a-cola!

20

Customer: Waiter! Call the manager—I can't eat this stew!
Waiter: *It's no use, sir. The manager won't eat it either.*

21

QUESTION OF THE MOMENT:
How do you cut through the waves?

Saint Patrick's Day

World Deep Sea Diving Day

ANSWER OF THE MOMENT:
With a sea-saw!

March

22 Why will you never starve in the desert?

Because of the sand which is there!

23 What's enormous, white, fluffy and hangs from the rafters of the bakery just outside the zoo?

24 What's large, gray and comes in four paper bags?

25 Today should be filled with eggsitement for you! Do eggsactly as you please. It's a great day for good yolks.

International Egg Day

26 How did the Eskimos get around town?

27 Did you hear about the cat that got hit by a bus?

28 What did the baby porcupine say when it backed into a cactus?

"Is that you, mother?"

Be Kind to Porcupines Day

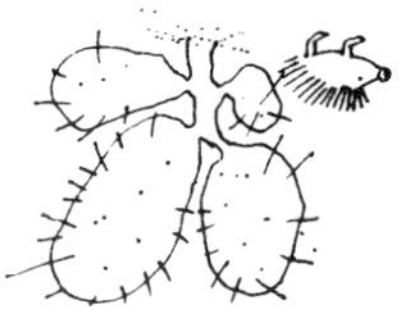

Yes, he had that rundown feeling.

On an icicle made for two!

A gift-wrapped elephant!

A meringue-outan!

March

29 What goes da-da-da-croak, dot-dot-croak, da-dot-da-croak?

30 The good thing about a dogwood is that its bark is worse than its bite!

31 "I believe in getting to the bottom of things," said the angry father as he spanked his naughty son.

A Morse toad!

April

1 What do you call an egg that loves April fools?

April Fools' Day

2 Why isn't a nose twelve inches long?

3 **Jack:** Dad, that dentist wasn't painless like he said he was.
Dad: *Why? Did he hurt you?*
Jack: No, but he screamed when I bit his finger, just like any other dentist.

4 What did the disappointed fencer say to his friend?

5 What do you call high-rise apartments for pigs?

6 Why is it dangerous to leave a clock at the top of the stairs?

7 Which is the oldest tree?

The elder.

Ostrich Day

Because it might run down!

Styscrapers!

Foiled again!

Because then it would be a foot!

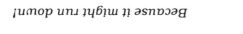

A practical yolker!

April

8

STREET SIGN OF THE MONTH:
To avoid that rundown feeling, look both ways before crossing.

9

Explorer: Why are you looking at me like that?

Cannibal: *Because I'm the food inspector.*

10

When is a ship not a ship?

11

Did you hear about Davy Crockett's three ears? His right ear, his left ear and his wild frontier!

12

Did you hear what the bulletin board said this morning?

13

Why did the chicken go only halfway across the road?

She wanted to lay it on the line!

14

When do your teeth resemble your tongue?

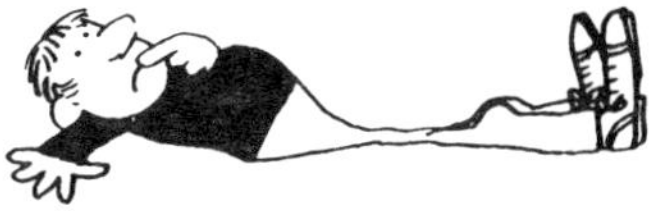

National Panic Week

When it's afloat!

"You can't pin anything on me."

When they start to chatter!

April

15

What's the best way to get in touch with a fish?

16

Waiter: How did you find the pork chop, sir?
Diner: *By accident—I moved the French fry and there it was!*

17

NEWS FLASH:
A dry cleaner was excused from jury duty yesterday because he said his business was pressing.

18

First tramp: Why did the elephant cross the road?
Second tramp: *Because it was the chicken's day off!*

19

What is the difference between an elephant and a flea?

20

Bill: What did you give your mom for her birthday?
Ben: *A 14-carrot necklace.*

21

HORRID RIDDLE OF THE WEEK:
Why shouldn't a pig get sick?

Because he'll have to be killed before he can be cured.

An elephant can have fleas, but a flea can't have an elephant.

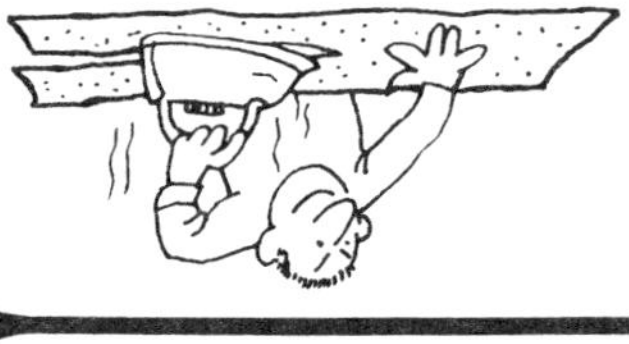

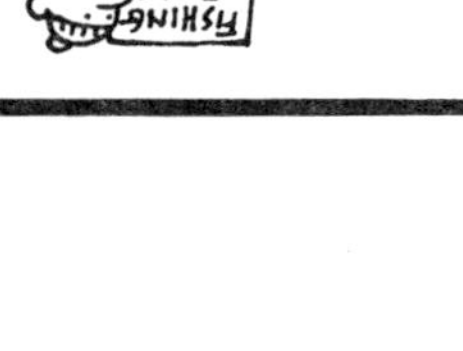

Drop it a line!

April

22

Willy: With what two animals do you always go to bed?
Billy: *Two calves!*

23

Businessman: How is your typing speed coming along, Miss Smith?
Miss Smith: *Oh, fine, thank you. Now I can make twenty mistakes a minute.*

24

Patient: I feel funny, doctor. What should I do?
Doctor: *Become a comedian!*

25

NEWS FLASH:
A man walked through midtown New York today wearing only a newspaper. He told police that he always likes to dress with *The Times*.

26

BOOK OF THE WEEK:
"Baby Sitting" by Justin Casey Howells.

27

Why couldn't the orange run downhill?

28

Shall I tell you the joke about the pencil?

National Secretaries Week

Because it had run out of juice!

No, there's no point to it.

April

29 I nearly got run over in my best pants. Luckily, I was able to get them off before the bus hit me.

30 What did the toothpaste say to the toothbrush?

"Give me a squeeze and I'll meet you outside."

May

1 Today's the day they crown the May Queen. As a prize they give her a book about May in the country. It's by Theresa Greene.

2 **Doctor:** Are you still taking the cough mixture I gave you?
Patient: *No. I tasted it once and decided I'd rather have the cough.*

3 Did you hear about the unhappy compass?

4 What do you get when you drop a grand piano down a mine shaft?

5 And what do you get when you drop a grand piano on an army barracks?

6 **NEWS FLASH:**
A strawberry was reported this afternoon to be in a bad jam.

7 What can you give away and still keep?

A cold!

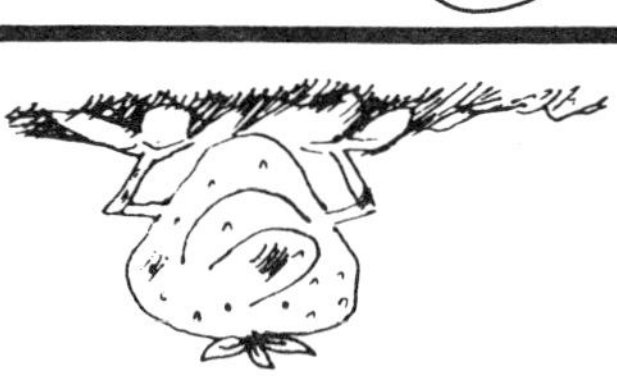

You get A Flat Major!

You get A Flat Minor!

It complained that it was always going around in circles.

May Day

May

8

You can dress up in anything you like this week—but don't go as far as the eye doctor's daughter did. She made a spectacle of herself.

9

Did you hear about the boy that some people thought was a tired dog?

They were confused by his short pants.

10

Jill: Look at that broken-down old shack. I wonder what keeps it together?
Jack: *The termites are holding hands.*

11

Why should fish be better educated than frogs?

12

NEWS FLASH:
Ten tons of human hair were stolen from a New York wig-maker today. Police are now combing the area.

13

Hickory dickory dock,
Two mice ran up the clock.
The clock struck one—
But the other got away.

14

"Tough luck," said the egg in the monastery. "It's out of the frying pan and into the Friar."

Daffy Dressing Up Week

Because fish live in schools!

May

15 Have you ever thought how parents spend the first part of a child's life encouraging him to walk and talk, and the rest of his childhood telling him to sit down and be quiet?

16 What are assets?

17 Why is the hot dog the noblest of all animals?

18 Why is a promise like an egg?

Because both are so easily broken!

19 How do you make a Maltese cross?

20 **Joe:** Did you hear the joke about the rotten eggs?
Jim: *No.*
Joe: Two bad!

21 **Little Dilly:** Mommy, what's a weapon?
Mother: *Something you fight with.*
Little Dilly: Is Daddy your weapon?

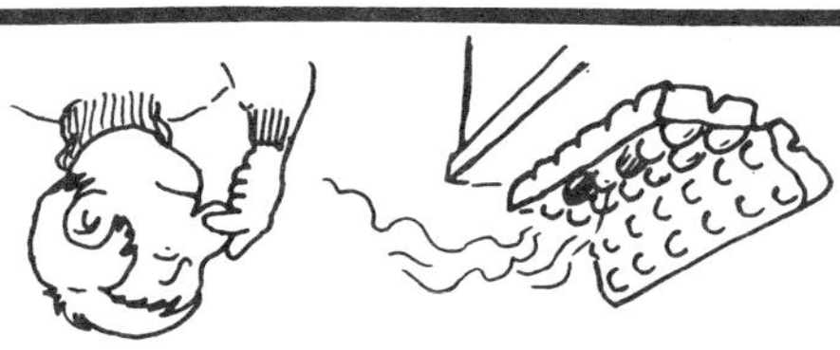

Stamp on his toe!

International Pickle Week

Because it feeds the hand that bites it!

Small donkeys!

May

22 What's the world's most shocking city?

23 **Man:** Do you think pineapples are happy?
Other man: *Well, I've never heard one complain.*

24 NEWS FLASH:
Yesterday a thousand men walked out of a steel mill while it was still in operation. They said they decided to strike while the iron was hot.

25 What do you give sick rabbits?

26 What goes uphill and downhill, but always stays in the same place?

27 **Doctor:** Don't you know my hours are from 9 until 12?

Patient: *Yes, but the mad dog that bit me didn't.*

28 QUESTION OF THE WEEK:
What vegetable needs a plumber?

Electricity!!

Hare tonic!

A road!

ANSWER OF THE WEEK:
The leek!

May

29

John: If you had only one match and you went into a room where there was a candle, a gas lamp and a stove, what would you light first?

Jill: *The candle.*

John: No, the match!

30

It's easy enough to be happy
When life goes merrily round,
But the man worthwhile
Is the man who can smile
When his pants are falling down!

31

Did you hear about the Russian cattle breeder?

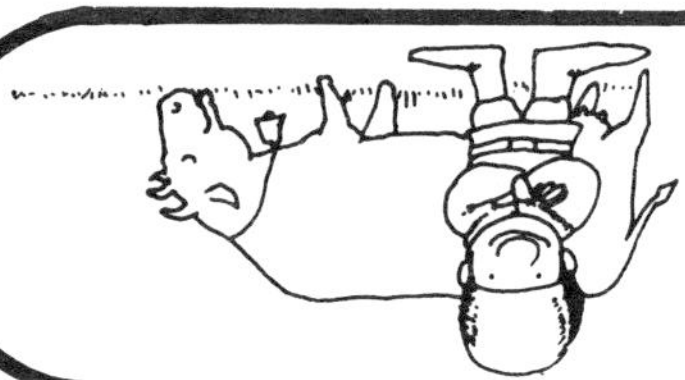

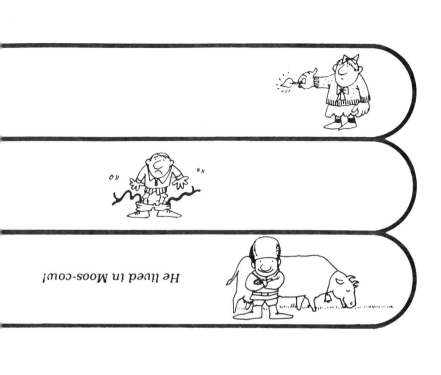

He lived in Moos-cow!

June

1

Dentist: Please stop screaming. I haven't even touched your tooth yet.
Patient: *I know, but you're standing on my foot.*

2

NEWS FLASH:

A dumpling was reported this morning to be in a big stew.

3

QUESTION OF THE MONTH:

How many balls of string would it take to reach from the earth to the moon?

4

Bill: Why is it dangerous to play cards in the jungle?
Ben: *Because of all the cheetahs!*

5

What does your watch say?

6

Have you heard about the new surgeon doll?

You just wind it up and it operates on batteries!

7

What does a lamb become after it is one year old?

Fight the Filthy Fly Month

ANSWER OF THE MONTH:
Only one if it was long enough.

Tick tock!

Two years old.

June

8 Could an elephant smell without his trunk?

9 How can you tell if there's an elephant in the refrigerator?

By the footprints in the butter.

10 How can you get five elephants into a compact car?

You can't. You could probably get two in the front and two in the back, but the fifth elephant would definitely have to walk.

11 What did the grape say when the elephant stepped on it?

12 How does an elephant get down from a tree?

13 How does an elephant get down from a tree?

It doesn't. It gets down from a duck.

14 Why are elephants flat-footed?

Because they're always jumping up and down with pleasure at hearing all those dreadful elephant jokes!

It climbs onto a leaf and waits till fall.

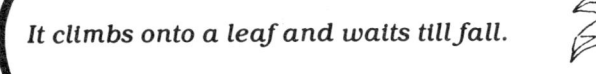

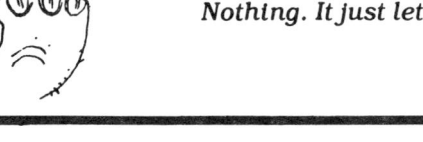

Nothing. It just let out a little whine.

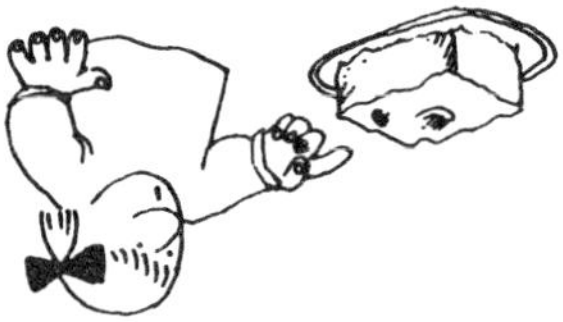

Yes, he'd still smell!

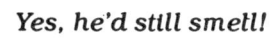

June

15

Bill: What's the best thing to put in a pie?
Ben: *Your teeth!*

16

What happens when you cross a giant elk with a pound of cocoa powder?

17

What did the frankfurter say to the ketchup?

That's enough of your sauce!

18

RIDDLE OF THE WEEK:
What words can be pronounced quicker and shorter by adding another syllable to them?

19

Sam: Where does a ghost-train stop?
Sally: *At a manifestation!*

20

Knock knock!
Who's there?
William.
William who?
Williamind your own business!

21

QUESTION OF THE DAY:
What do you call pigs that like each other?

You get a chocolate moose!

Fudge-Off Finals

QUICK and SHORT.

Make a Face Day

ANSWER OF THE MINUTE:
Pen pals!

June

22

Will: Why can only very small gnomes and elves sit underneath toadstools?
Jill: *Because there is not mushroom!*

23

Bob: Who always goes to sleep with his shoes on?
Tom: *I don't know. Who?*
Bob: A horse!

24

Why did the elephant leave the circus?

25

When is a door not a door?

26

NEWS FLASH:
The President of the International Periscope Manufacturers Association said today that business was looking up.

27

Did you hear what happened to the two burglars who stole a calendar?

28

What's big, hairy and flies at 2000 m.p.h.?

National Fink Day

He got tired of working for peanuts!

When it is ajar!

They each got six months.

King Kongcorde!

June

29 Why do elephants wear slippers?

30 What did the little kid call his pet leopard?

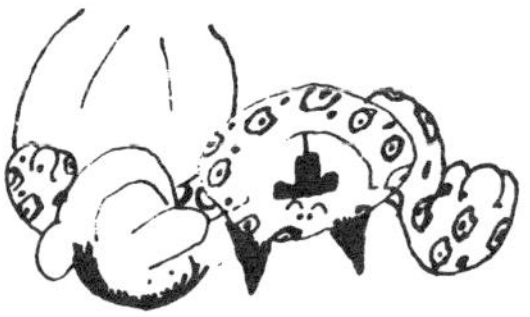

Spot.

So they can sneak up on mice without being heard.

July

1

Mick: Teacher, I et seven eggs for breakfast.
Teacher: *Ate, Mick, ate.*
Mick: It might have been eight, but I know I et an awful lot.

2

THOUGHT OF THE WEEK:
A graveyard is never deserted. You are always sure to find some body there.

3

RIDDLE OF THE WEEK:
What did the beaver say to the tree?

4

What do you do with sick birds?

Independence Day

5

If a man smashed a grandfather clock, could he be accused of killing time?

6

What do you do with a wombat?

7

My mother always believed in germ-free food. She used to put arsenic in my sandwiches to make sure she killed them.

Play wom, of course!

Not if the clock struck first.

Have them tweeted.

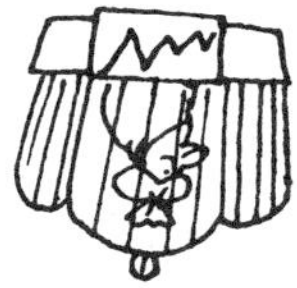

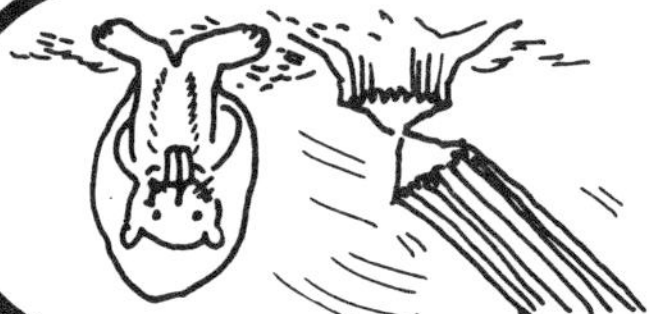

It was nice gnawing you!

July

8

SIGN OF THE TIMES:

Cross Roads

(Better humor them)

9

Sam: I had a fall last night that kept me unconscious for nearly nine hours.
Jim: *Oh dear, where did you fall?*
Sam: I fell asleep.

10

What does a queen do when she burps?

11

"Did you hear what that carpet said to the floor today?"

12

Why are a pastry cook's hands like a July garden?

13

Sunday school teacher: As you know, all the animals that came to Noah's ark came in pairs.
Tommy: *That's not true. The two worms came in apples.*

14

A LITTLE BIT OF HISTORY:

At the time of the French Revolution many people lost their heads . . .

Bastille Day

Noah's Birthday

Both are in flower (flour)!

"Don't move. I've got you covered."

She issues a royal pardon!

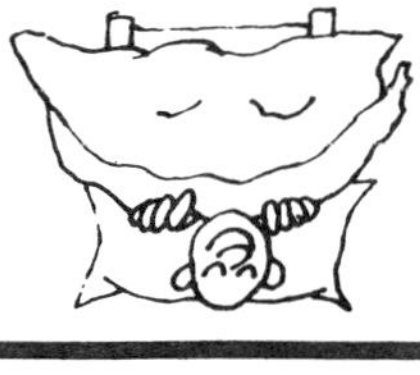

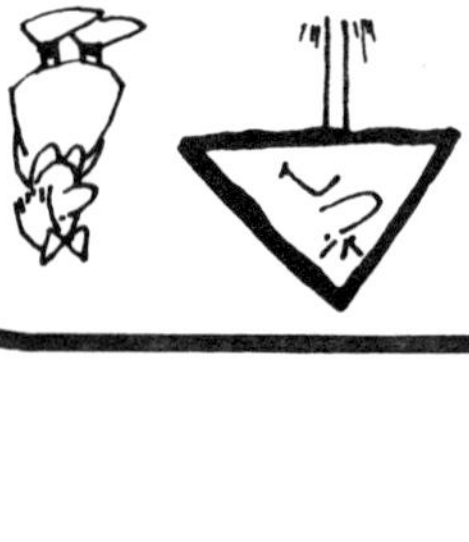

July

15

BOOKS OF THE MONTH:
"The Dog's Dinner" by Nora Bone
"How to Be a Track Star" by Arthur Letics
"Rugs" by Walter Wall

16

QUESTION OF THE DAY:
Where do baby beans come from?

17

Ladies and gentlemen, meet Anna Sthetic! This girl's a real knock-out!

18

Notice to be placed in all gardens in July:
"Anyone is welcome to come and borrow our lawn mower, as long as he doesn't take it out of our garden."

19

Phil: You know, I always get up when the first ray of sunlight hits my window.
Jill: *Isn't that rather early?*
Phil: No. My room faces west.

20

What is very beautiful, sits on flowers and is highly dangerous?

A man-eating butterfly!

21

Who are the world's three unluckiest ladies?

ANSWER OF THE HOUR:
They are brought by the stalk!

Miss Chance
Miss Fortune
Miss Hap

July

22 Oscar McTavish was a man after my own heart. He tried to stab me in the chest this morning.

23 **Dad:** How do you like going to school, Jimmy?
Jimmy: *I like going to school, Dad. And I like coming home from school. It's the time in between I hate.*

24 How did the man-eating tiger feel after he had eaten a whole pillow?

25 I've always believed in love at first sight—ever since I first looked into a mirror.

26 **Secretary:** The Invisible Man is waiting for you, sir.
Boss: *Tell him I can't see him.*

27 **Teacher (answering telephone):** You say Johnny Johnson has a bad cold and can't come to school today. To whom am I speaking?
Voice: *Oh, this is my father.*

28 Did you hear about the human cannonball at the circus?

Down in the mouth!

Be Kind to Tadpoles Day

He got fired.

July

29

A man was working in a butcher shop. He was six feet tall and wore size 10 shoes. What did he weigh?
I don't know.
Meat!

30

How many sides does a circle have?
A circle doesn't have sides.
Yes, it does. The inside and the outside!

31

Bill: What's the difference between a tuna fish and a grand piano?
Ben: *I don't know.*
Bill: You can't tune a fish!

ACE
PIANO
TUNING

August

1

Why did the man with only one hand cross the road?

To get to the second-hand store!

2

What's in the middle of Paris, five hundred yards tall and always wet?

3

There's only one flower that grows on your face—tulips!

Nonsense! I've got roses in my cheeks.

4

I often go for a tramp in the woods in August. Fortunately for the tramp I don't often find him.

Lizzie Borden Liberation Day

5

BOOKS OF THE MONTH:

"Easy Money" by Robin Banks
"The Great Descent" by Aileen Dover
"Time for Food" by Dean R. Bell

6

There's only one way to get into a locked cemetery at night. You use a skeleton key.

7

Lucy: Mother, my teacher punished me for something I didn't do.
Mother: *What was that, dear?*
Lucy: My homework!

The Eiffel Shower!

August

8

Tall, fat man in the movie theatre to little boy sitting behind him: Can you see, sonny?
Little boy: *No.*
Man: Don't worry. Just laugh when I do.

9

Where does it cost $50 a head to eat?

10

When asked to make a contribution to the local orphanage, my friend Sheila sent two orphans.

11

I have four legs, but only one foot. What am I?

12

What goes Ho Ho Ho Bonk?

The Green Giant laughing his head off!

13

Tim: What did the lovesick moon-boy say to the lovesick moon-girl?
Tom: *Oh, how romantic! There's a beautiful full-earth out tonight!*

14

What is salty, greasy and makes you unhappy?

International Have-a-Potato-Chip-Today Day

A chip on the shoulder.

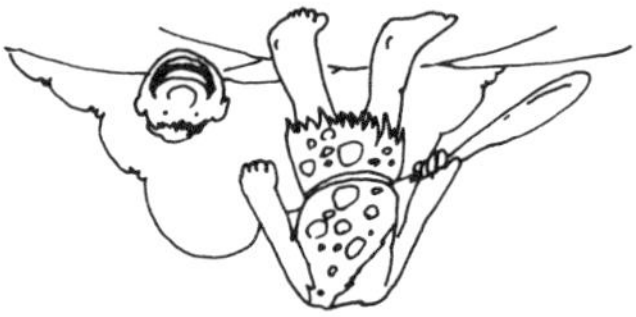

A bed.

In the Cannibal Cafe.

August

15 This is World Sing a Hymn Day. (If you object to singing hymns, sing hers instead.)

16 Who was the cowboy who had the twelve guns and terrorized the ocean bed?

17 You know that owls never feel romantic when it's been raining. That's when they sit on the branches of the trees where they live and call out, "Too wet to woo! Too wet to woo!"

18 What wears shoes, but has no feet?

19 **Nervous passenger:** Do these planes crash often?
Air hostess: *Only once.*

20 Did you hear about Romeo and Juliet? They met in a revolving door—and they've been going around together ever since.

Romeo and Juliet's Anniversary

21 How could you go without sleep for seven whole nights and still not be tired?

By sleeping through the days.

The pavement!

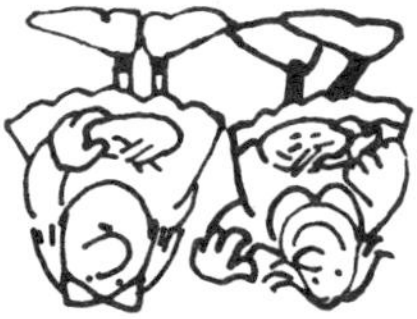

Billy the Squid!

August

22

Ron: Do insects have brains?
Edna: *Of course, insects have brains. How else do you think they'd figure out where we were going to have our picnic!*

23

THOUGHT OF THE MONTH:
The cheapest time to phone your friends is . . . when they're out!

24

If I put a dozen ducks into this old wooden box what will I have?

25

What do you get when you cross a sheep with a thunderstorm?

26

How did the philosopher manage to get the elephant across the Atlantic without using a boat or a plane?

27

Ned: What's the world's fastest drink?
Jed: *Milk—because it's pasteurized before you see it!*

28

Have you heard about the latest development in gardening? People are getting cows to cut the grass. They call them Lawn Moo-ers!

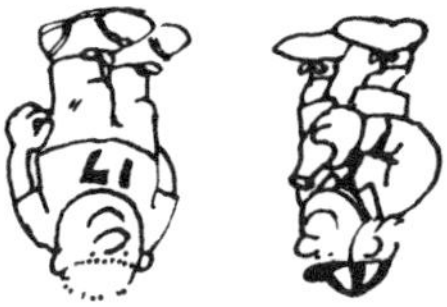

He just thought it over!

A wet blanket!

A box of quackers.

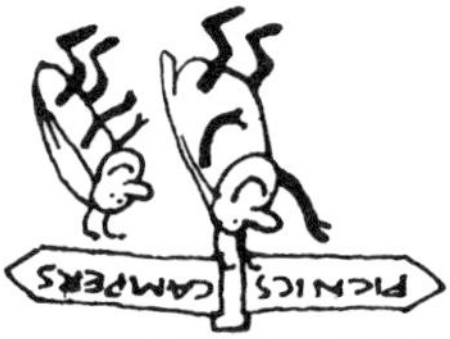

August

29 When witches brew tea, they drink it out of cups and sorcerers.

Try a Cup of Tea Day

30 **Jack:** I weighed only three pounds when I was born.
Jill: *Did you live?*
Jack: Did I live! You should see me now.

31 There were three men in a boat with four cigarettes but no matches. You'll never believe what they did. They threw out one cigarette and made the boat a cigarette lighter!

September

1

"Oh, Doris, I'm so sorry to hear your uncle died in a barrel of varnish. What a way to go!"

"It's all right—he had a beautiful finish."

2

Master of Disguise: You know, this isn't my own mustache I'm wearing. My real one's in my pocket.

Mustache Day

3

Why does an ill-mannered Communist called Alfred always stay indoors during wet weather?

Because Rude Alf, the Red, knows Rain, Dear!

4

Ron: Mom, all the boys at school called me a girl!
Mom: *What did you do, dear?*
Ron: Hit them with my handbag!

5

Jack: Is your electric toaster a pop-up model?
Jill: *No, it's an Indian model.*
Jack: What's that?

6

Billy: Do you mean to tell me you fell over fifty feet and didn't get hurt?
Sally: *Yes. I was just trying to get to the back of the bus.*

7

What do you call the man who owns all the cows in Arabia?

Be Late for Something Day

International
Cheer Day

Jill: *A toaster that sends up smoke signals.*

The milk shaikh!

September

8

QUESTION OF THE WEEK:
How can you recognize a dogwood tree?

ANSWER OF THE YEAR:
By its bark.

9

What do cats read every morning?
Mewspapers.
And gnus?
Gnuspapers!

10

I learned to swim at a very early age. My parents used to row me out to the middle of a lake and drop me in the water so that I had to swim to the shore on my own. The swim was easy. It was getting out of the sack that was difficult.

11

When you look around on a very cold day, what do you see on every hand?

12

Mother Chick: What do you want for breakfast?
Baby Chick: *Shredded tweet!*

13

What has six feet and sings?

14

THINGS YOU NEVER SAW:
A shoe box!
A salad bowl!
A square dance!

A trio!

A glove.

September

15

Teacher: How do you spell "scarecrow"?
Pupil: *S-K-A-R-K-R-O.*
Teacher: The dictionary spells it S-C-A-R-E-C-R-O-W.
Pupil: *You didn't ask me how the dictionary spells it!*

16

Why can't two elephants go into the sea at the same time?

Because between them they have only one pair of trunks!

17

GREAT SAYINGS OF OUR TIME:
"I love kids. I used to go to school with them."

18

Why is a lord like a book?

Because they both have a title.

19

Young Agricultural Student: Your methods of cultivation are very old-fashioned. For example, I'd be very surprised if you got more than six pounds of apples from that tree.
Old Farmer: *So would I. It's a cherry tree.*

20

What do misers do during a chilly September?

21

In prehistoric times, what did they call ship disasters at sea?

National Hop Up & Down Day

Sit around a candle!

Tyrannosaurus Wrecks!

September

22

Scout leader: You're facing North. On your left is West. On your right is East. What's at your back?
Scout: *My sleeping bag!*

23

Little Rodney: Oh, Mom, I feel as sick as a dog.
Mother: *Don't worry, dear. I'll call the vet.*

National Dog Week

24

What kind of boats do vampires like?

Sleep Under the Bed Tonight Night

25

Teacher: Switzerland is as big as Siam. Now, George, are you paying attention? How big is Switzerland?
George: *As big as you are.*

26

"Where's your pencil, Roy?" "I ain't got none." "How many times do I have to tell you? It's I haven't got one. You haven't got one. We haven't got one. They haven't got one." *"Well, where are all the pencils then if nobody ain't got none?"*

27

In a race, what does the winner lose?

His breath.

World Run-A-Mile Day

28

The Punk Rock group threw a stick of dynamite into the middle of the audience. That really brought the house down.

Blood vessels!

September

29 The surgeon cleared his throat—by removing his tonsils, adenoids, tongue, teeth and gums.

30 What's the difference between a wizard and the letters M, A, K, E, S?

One makes spells and the other spells makes!

PABCDEFGHIJK

October

1

Soldiers mark time with their feet. What does the same thing with its hands?

A clock!

2

My grandfather used to think he was a canary. But he went to a marvelous psychiatrist and now we don't hear a peep out of him.

3

NEWS FLASH:
Earlier today the chairmen of two swimming pool companies were having a heated argument.

4

Jane: I had a parrot for five years. It never said a word.
Lucy: *Was it shy?*
Jane: No, it was stuffed!

5

POLICE NOTICE
Man wanted for burglary. Apply inside.

6

Doctor: And what's that old miser complaining about now?
Nurse: *He says he got better long before that medicine you gave him was all used up.*

7

QUESTION OF THE WEEK:
What would be the best thing to do if you decided you were mad?

October is International Berry Month

ANSWER OF THE WEEK:
Change your mind!

October

8

Why did the cyclist leave the race?

He was forced to retire!

9

How do you make anti-freeze?

10

Lord Ptolemy Ffitch-Fitzwilliams was born with a silver spoon in his mouth. Once it was taken out, he was all right.

11

What's the secret of being a great choirboy?

12

John: Can you think of a bus that has crossed the Atlantic?
Jill: *Yes. Columbus.*

13

What's a volcano?

A mountain with the hiccups!

14

HORRID RIDDLE OF THE WEEK:
What has four legs and flies?

A dead horse!

Columbus Day

B natural!

Stick her in the refrigerator!

October

15 **RIDICULOUS RIDDLE OF THE WEEK:**
If your mother was born in Iceland and your father was born in Cuba, what are you?

16 What part of London is in France?

17 What should you call a hairless koala?

18 Sensible people always carry olive oil around with them—just in case they bump into a squeaky olive.

19 When is an opera singer not an opera singer?

20 **Willy:** Hey, Mom, the garbage man is at the door.
Mom: *Tell him we don't want any.*

21 **Fatty:** I'm disgusted.
Friend: *Why?*
Fatty: I stepped onto the Speak-Your-Weight scale today and it said, "One person at a time, please."

When he's a little hoarse.

Fred Bear!

The letter N!

An ice cube!

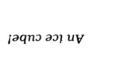

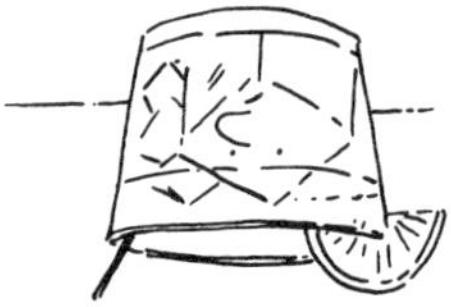

October

22

Jenny: Aren't you rather hot doing all that painting dressed like that?
Ginny: *Well, it says here on the paint can to be sure to put on at least two coats!*

23

"Waiter, what's this fly doing in my soup?"

"It looks like the backstroke to me, sir!"

24

Little girl showing her friend the scale in the bathroom: "All I know is that you stand on it and it makes you furious."

25

My father was a very religious man, you know. He wouldn't work if there was a Sunday in the week.

National Pretzel Week

26

Why do cows like lying on sunny beaches?

27

Tax Inspector: As a good citizen you should pay your taxes with a smile.
Businessman: *That's what I want to do, but you keep asking for money!*

28

"Don't you think that new overcoat of yours is a bit loud?"

"It'll be all right when I put on a muffler."

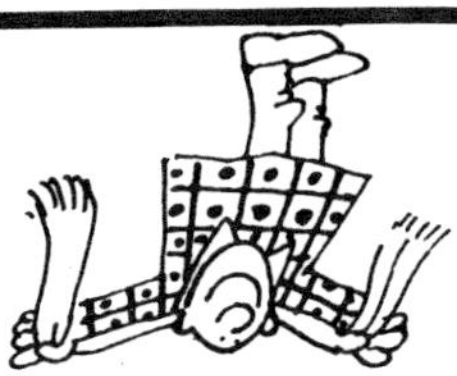

Because they enjoy tanning their hides.

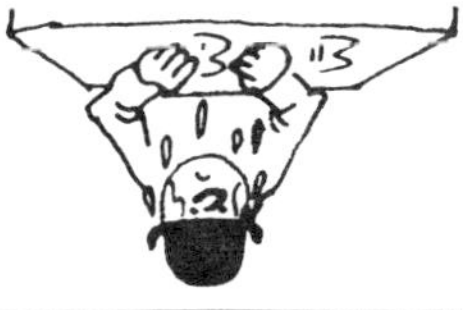

October

29

"I went to the theatre last night, but I left after the first act."
"Why?"
"It said on the program: Act Two—Five Years Later. I couldn't wait that long."

30

What do ghosts have for dinner?

31

Max: I think your school must be haunted.
Jim: *Why do you think that?*
Max: Well, your principal is always talking about school spirit.

Halloween

Spooketti!

November

1

"When is a man-eating tiger most likely to enter a house?"
"I don't know. When?"
"When the door's open!"

2

Mother: Now, Judy, you know you're not supposed to eat with your knife.
Judy: *Yes, Mom, but my fork leaks!*

3

What goes croak-croak when it's misty?

4

Patient: I'm so worried. I keep thinking I'm a pair of drapes.
Doctor: *Don't worry and pull yourself together!*

5

Guy: Can you spell Blind Pig?
Mrs. Guy: *B-L-I-N-D P-I-G.*
Guy: Wrong. It's B-L-N-D P-G. With two I's he wouldn't be blind.

6

How did the Mexican detective know that Juan Dominguez had been killed with a Golf Gun?

7

To what regiment in the army do baby soldiers belong?

The infantry!

Because it had definitely made a hole in Juan!

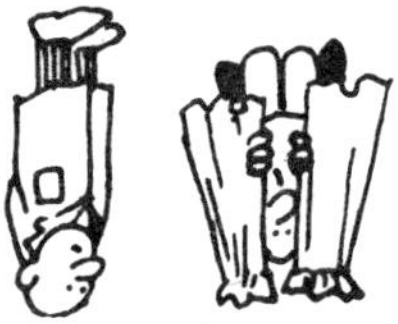

A frog-horn!

November

8

Bill: Ouch! That water's just burned my hand.
Ben: *Well, silly, you should have felt it before putting your hand in.*

9

How should you dress on a cold day?

Quickly!

10

Mrs. McDonald's son, Ronald, went off to join the army. After six months he wrote to her to say he'd grown another foot. So, sensible woman, she knitted him another sock.

11

"You know the best kind of paper to use when you're making a kite?"
"No, what?"
"Flypaper!"

12

What did the mother bee call the baby bee?

13

Did you hear about the little boy who went to the street corner to watch the traffic jam?

A truck came along and gave him a jar.

14

Harry: I'm going to buy a farm two hundred miles long and half an inch wide.
Barry: *What on earth are you going to grow?*
Harry: Spaghetti!

Her little humbug!

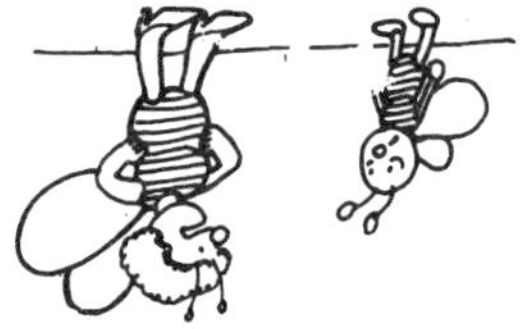

November

15

"What is French for 'I am an Australian'?"
"I don't know. What?"
"'Moi Aussi.'"

16

Have you heard about the woman who was afraid she was dying?

She went and sat in the living room and felt a lot better.

17

Wee Willy wrote at the end of second grade:
"Miss Hoskins, I like you so much. I'm sorry you're not bright enough to teach us next year when we're in third grade."

18

Did you hear about the people who moved into the city because the country was at war?

19

What did one bay say to the other bay?

20

I've just realized why Robin Hood only robbed the rich. He knew the poor didn't have anything.

21

What's a frog spy called?

A croak-and-dagger agent.

"Show us your mussels!"

November

22

Minnie: My grandma can play the piano by ear.
Mickey: *That's nothing. My grandad fiddles with his whiskers.*

23

"What's on the TV tonight, Sal?"

24

"I slept very badly last night, you know."
"Really? Why?"
"Well, I plugged my electric blanket into the toaster by mistake and I spent the whole night popping out of bed."

25

QUESTION OF THE MONTH:
If the plug doesn't fit, do you socket?

26

"I'm afraid I've just run over your cat. I'm so sorry. Can I replace it?

"That's very nice of you, but do you think you'll be able to catch mice?"

27

Repair Man: I've come to repair your doorbell.
Mrs. Jones: *But you were supposed to have come yesterday.*
Repair Man: I did. I rang the bell five times and got no answer.

28

Why don't elephants ride bicycles?

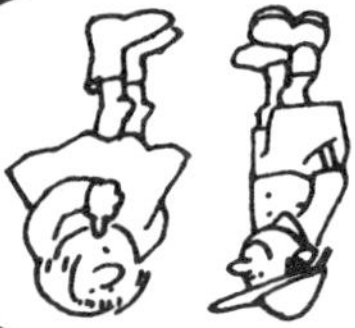

Because their thumbs can't work the bell.

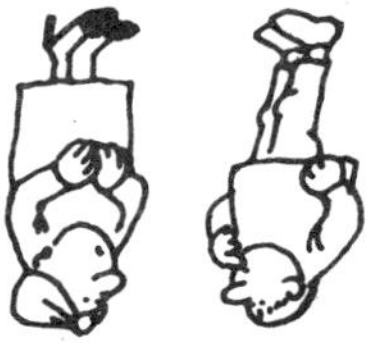

"Same as usual, Sam—the goldfish bowl and an ashtray."

November

29 What should a mother do if her son swallows a pen?

Use a pencil till the doctor arrives.

30 When is the best time to buy parakeets?

When they're going cheep!

December

1

Joe: Did you hear the joke about the rope?
Jack: *No.*
Joe: Then let's skip it.

2

SIGN OUTSIDE A HAIRSTYLIST'S:
WE CURL UP AND DYE FOR YOU!

3

Mom: Johnny, have you given the goldfish fresh water today?
Johnny: *No, Mom. He hasn't drunk what I gave him yesterday.*

4

NEWS FLASH:
Late last night a huge hole was cut in the wooden fence surrounding St. Vitus's Nudist Camp. The authorities are looking into it.

5

What ship has no captain but two mates?

6

Mr. and Mrs. Smith had just adopted a little baby girl who came to them from France. At the same time they started taking French lessons so that they'd know what the baby was saying as soon as it began to talk.

7

RIDDLE OF THE WEEK:
Why did the thief take a shower?

So he could make a clean getaway.

Courtship!

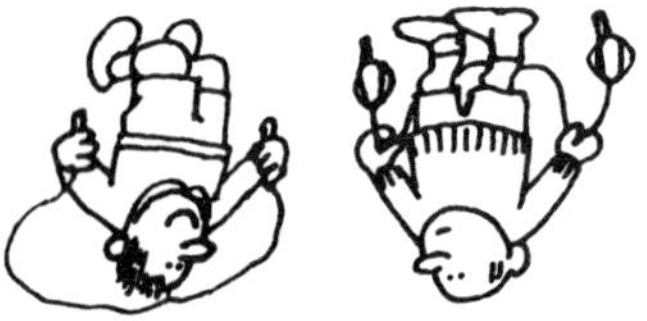

December

8

Once upon a time there was a little boy called Merlin. He was an amazing magician. He went around a corner and turned into a candy store.

9

There's a new kind of soap on the market. It's ten feet high and four feet wide. Instead of lifting it up to wash with, you lie on it and slide up and down!

10

Why was the farmer unhappy?

Because someone stepped on his corn.

National Bricklayers' Day

11

Why is it always cold at football games?

12

Some people are so shy, they have to go into a dark room just to change their minds.

National Ding-A-Ling Day

13

Adam: And I shall call that creature a hippopotamus.
Eve: *But why, dear?*
Adam: Because it *looks* like a hippopotamus, of course!

14

Here's one way to put yourself through a keyhole. Write "yourself" on a tiny piece of paper and pass it through the keyhole!

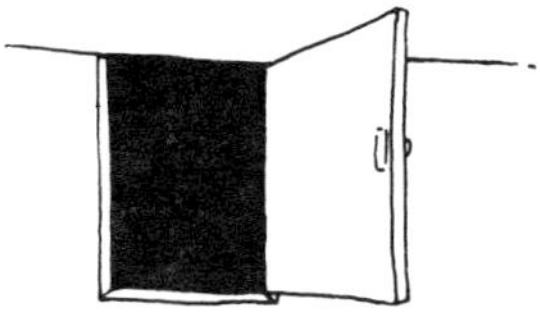

Because of all the fans that are there!

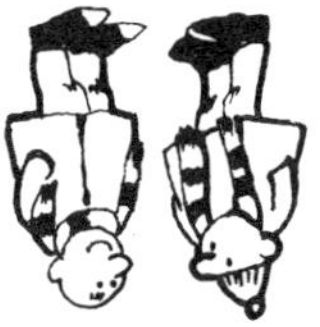

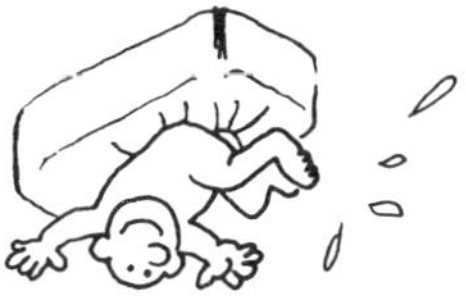

December

15 What is the best way to avoid falling hair?

16 Why did the girl put her bed in the fireplace?

17 **Tim (answering telephone):** Hello.
Voice: *Hello. Is Boo there?*
Tim: Boo who?
Voice: *Don't cry, little boy. I must have got the wrong number.*

18 What goes in dry, comes out wet and pleases people?

19 What musical instrument can be used for fishing?

20 "What should you do if you split your sides laughing?"
"I don't know. What?"
"Run until you get a stitch in them!"

21 Where should two motorists have a swordfight?

On a dual highway, of course!

A cast-a-net!

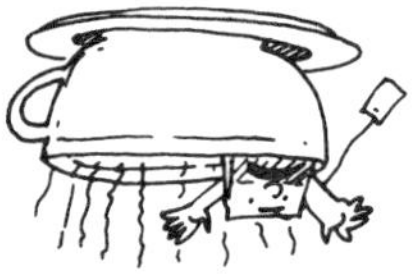

A tea bag!

Because she wanted to sleep like a log.

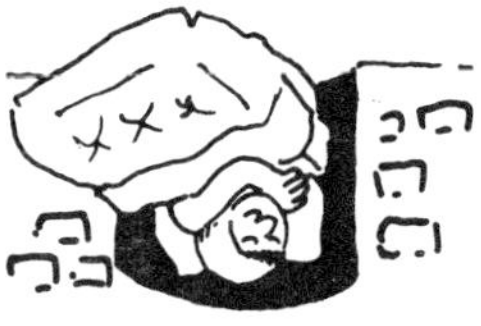

Jump out of the way!

December

22 SIGN IN A GOLF CLUB:
BACK SOON. GONE TO TEE.

23 NEWS FLASH:
Yesterday a lady dropped her handbag over the edge of the railroad platform. The porters refused to go get the bag as they considered it beneath their station.

24 What do you call a tug of war on December 24th?

25 Who is Santa Claus's wife?

Mary Christmas.

Christmas Day

26 What's the Christmas song monkeys like best?

27 **Jill:** There are several things I can always count on.
Jack: *What are they?*
Jill: My fingers.

28 What do Eskimos call the big, formal dances they have at Christmas?

Snowballs!
"Jungle Bells"!
Christmas Heave!
CLOSED

December

29 Why aren't they going to grow bananas any longer?

30 How can you tell when there's an elephant under your bed?

31 What comes at the end of every year?

The letter R!

New Year's Eve

When your nose hits the ceiling!

Because they're long enough already!